ISIOMA J. OLELEH

Purpose: Your Map to Greatness

ISIOMA J. OLELEH

ISBN: 978-0-615-88587-2

ISIOMA J. OLELEH

PURPOSE: Your Map to Greatness

Dedication

I dedicate this book to everyone who is seeking to understand God's will for his/her life, and I pray that this book brings you closer to that answer in Jesus' name.

Amen

To be great is to be used as God`s hands and feet on this earth. Great people are positioned to do exploits in their generation using their skills, talents and abilities. Do you dare to become great?

If yes, join me on a journey as you discover and map out your purpose!

If you have ever asked yourself, "Why am I here on the earth?" Then, you are just like me. I wondered for many years, I soon realized that I was made for something GREAT!

- **GROWTH**
- **RESOURCES**
- **ENERGY**
- **ACQUIRE**
- **TREASURES**

AND YOU ARE TOO!

If any man seeks for greatness, let him forget greatness and ask for truth, and he will find both.

HORACE MANN

TABLE OF CONTENTS

PREFACE

Purpose is the most potent remedy to a fruitful life. Many people are searching for meaning, living less than their abilities because they don't know what and who they are. A discovery of purpose is the cure to every form of depression, hopelessness and stagnancy in life. When we discover our purpose it then infuses us with life, joy and creativity. Purpose is the map that leads us to greatness because every human being was made in the image of a great God whose wisdom and might is infinite. We were made to **GLORIFY** God, so how can we do this? We glorify him with our lives and by exhibiting his image in us to our world.

Seeds will always reproduce after their kind, so it is with human beings. As the apple has the genetic and physical composition of the seed that was placed in the ground, so were human beings created to have the same likeness and nature of God, and it is evident in the word of God that says, "Ye are gods, children of the most high God." Psalms 82: 6.

Before we were created, God had a plan in mind for our lives; a specific role that we are supposed to play and a path that was destined for each individual. "We are His workmanship, created in Him to do the good works which HE had already predestined for us before the beginning of time." Ephesians 2:10.

His purpose for us is the manual by which we run our lives; just as an unassembled furniture requires the right manual for it to serve the purpose for which it was acquired. God had a unique purpose for every life even before that life made it to the womb.

This purpose houses our treasures, makes us a blessing to people and leads us to a position of greatness where we will make tremendous impact and contributions to our world. In the purpose driven life, Rick Warren stated that one's purpose is not a product of research or speculation but the calling of God which can be only be discovered through the understanding of the working of God in one's heart. God does not leave you in the dark concerning his work in your life.

We are the body of Christ and we play different roles based on the service we have rendered which will be dependent on the assignment and potentials he has given each one of us. We are all created for greatness, which thus demands that we become uncomfortable living miserably and dying like servants; whereas we are kings and queens made to sit in palaces and influence the earth positively. When we discover God's plan and map it out, it will lead us to greatness!

Foreword

There is a "good life" that God has prearranged and made ready for everyone on earth to live. The terms and conditions are the blocking barriers between each person and the "good life." These terms and conditions are well spelled out in the book of Ephesians 2:10 (amplified version) as (1) recreation, (2) doing the predestined good works, and (3) taking prepared paths. "For we are God's [own] handiwork (His workmanship), recreated in Christ Jesus, [born anew] that we may do those good works which God predestined (planned beforehand) for us [taking paths which He prepared ahead of time], that we should walk in them [living the good life which He prearranged and made ready for us to live.]"

This scripture best enumerates and illustrates a master piece of success principles; which is diligently and professionally packaged in this book by Ms. Isioma Oleleh. The beautiful part of this unfolding knowledge is the fact that Ms. Isioma is not just writing about a principle she studied in school or learned about at a success seminar. Rather, she is sharing a life she lives and a path she has been following over the years. I am a living support of this claim. There are two major reasons why people fail in life; (1) lack of knowledge of success principles, and (2) lack of discipline to apply them.

I believe that anyone who cares to learn the principles shared in this book and is diligent enough to apply them, stands over a 90% chance of succeeding in life. There are carefully extracted action points at the end of each chapter that make it easier to practice the principles taught in each chapter. Many people are uninformed, confused, or frustrated about their purpose on earth while many lack the strategy to accomplish it. The answers to all the aforementioned issues are clearly stated in this book. Ms. Isioma's consistency in her belief, progress in life, humility, obedience to authority, drive to see others succeed, and commitment to righteousness makes her more than competent to add to the body of knowledge in this subject area. I therefore encourage everyone not only to read this masterpiece, but to diligently hearken and observe to do all the principles stated therein. You will be glad you did!

Pastor Mike Adebiyi
Senior Pastor of JCCI HOG ATLANTA
President of Consortium for Africa Development (CAD)

Chapter 1

FINDING YOUR LOCATION

There are two great days in a person's life: the day we are born and the day we discover why.

William Barclay

Section 1

What is the location?

A group of people were asked to describe the word "map" in two words and the answers were as follows: "direction path," "destination locator," "land locator," and "treasure finder." These definitions imply that a map should either help one locate or follow a direction, destination, land, or treasure. Every one desires to be great; for many people it is the reason why they get up early in the morning to go to school, work or a business.

Thus, many equate success and stability with greatness. So what does it mean to be great? According to dictionary.com, it is an unusual degree, power or intensity. The word greatness means to possess such unusual power, degree and intensity. So how does a person attain greatness? Is there truly a location of greatness? Does it just happen to people of certain races or geographical backgrounds? No great person ever stumbled upon greatness but can rather be described as a journey. Autobiographies of great men tell the story of them visualizing the end of a journey and having an understanding of why they needed to press through the challenges they encountered before the vision came into reality. Those great men had an idea of where they were headed and a sense of purpose of why they were going there. Thus, it became their map to greatness. Many great men also discovered their purpose through a plethora of experiences, and others through a strong instinct that they were wired to accomplish that particular task.

For example, George Washington Carver was a slave who discovered his purpose as a result of the poverty he saw around him. He wanted poor farmers to grow alternative crops both as a source of their own food and as a source of other products to improve their quality of life. He developed 105 food recipes using peanuts and promoted about 100 products made from peanuts that were useful for the house and farm, including cosmetics, dyes, paints, plastics, gasoline, and nitroglycerin. He empowered many poor farmers to become financially independent.

Purpose can thus be defined as the reason for existence: the premise for which something exists. Jeremiah 1:5 states "Before I formed you, I knew you and sent you as a prophet to the nations." Before you were born, God had a purpose for your existence. You were not created to occupy space on this earth or just work a dead end job. There is actually something in you that no one else in the world can produce but you. In one's location of greatness, there is a natural attraction that pulls you to things related to your purpose; these things give us joy, pain, hope and courage. Like George Carver, in spite of your current situation, there is something in you waiting to be unleashed to your world.

You are wired to do great things in this world if only you discover the purpose for which you were created. There is a location waiting for your assignment, gifts, talents and treasures. You are created to do great things, don't miss the errand!

Section 2

How do I know when I have found my location?

The location of greatness is thus not a physical place but rather where the entirety of a person is fully expressed and engaged purposefully. In the areas of one's purpose, there is a tendacity to have clearer insight and wisdom about such areas. For example, someone who has been destined to become a voice in the financial world is able to notice trends in the financial sector that others might overlook. This person must also work hard to acquire knowledge about the trends in that sector, learn to become more diligent and have integrity over financial matters so as to make maximum impact.

There must be a desire to find the location of greatness, and it must be sought after because God has allocated great treasures in that land for the man. Young Oprah Winfrey, the wealthiest African American woman in media speaks of how she used to interview her dolls as a kid, today, her talk show and TV channel is being sought after globally. There is an instinctinal gravitation towards the areas related to our purpose, we naturally possess unusual wisdom in those areas.

In Exodus 31:2-6, God said to Moses, "See I have called him by name Bezaleel, the son of Uri, and I have filled him with the spirit of God, in wisdom, in understanding, and in knowledge and in all manner of workmanship to devise cunning works, to work in gold, silver, brass, in cutting of stones to set them and in carving of timber to work in all manners of workmanship." Bezaleel's assignment on this earth was carpentry and this can be defined as his purpose. God had given him the wisdom to devise excellent structures and by using that skill, he was able to create magnificent edifices like no one else.

Everyone has been endowed with tools for greatness because of the mandate given to Adam when God blessed him and said to him to be fruitful, multiply, replenish and subdue the earth (Genesis 1:28). HE also gave that command to Noah (Genesis 9:1) and Abraham (Genesis 16:6). Once an individual locates his land of greatness, he begins to fulfill the same mandate that was given to Noah and Abraham, which then attracts great treasures to him. God always has a purpose for blessing a man; HE bestows a gift on him and then assigns him a function, which will be used in the location that he finds. I believe one of Oprah's assignments was to be become a philanthropist. As she attained greatness with her role in media, she was able to fund her next assignment, which is to help people through several ventures.

Section 3

What do I do with this information?

After a person has discovered his purpose and identified possible locations of greatness, the person must then focus their thoughts on what they want to accomplish. The earth is like a magnet that attracts the most prevalent thoughts. If a person believes that they can achieve something, they mostly likely will. Our thoughts emit waves that transmit the corresponding signals back to you.

One of the ways to focus your thoughts is through the act of Meditation. Meditation is the process in which you quiet your mind, revitalize your thoughts which helps you come up with ideas and strategies to plan better. Meditation is better spent in solitude, it is a time of deep reflection where distractions are removed, strength and a stronger clarity of vision is regained. Meditating on an idea allows one to gain deep insight on different avenues of exploring that particular idea. After you begin to identify possible areas of one`s purpose, start to make practical steps to begin the journey toward greatness because plans without action is a display of lack of faith.

For example, George Washington Carver was a slave who was angered by the poverty of his community, he then had a vision to help himself and other farmers out of poverty which led him to create over a hundred things from the peanut.

As you discover your purpose and location of greatness, you must remember that greatness is progressive. It is a step by step journey and never a destination thus greatness is in stages and levels, one assignment leads to the other. One must continue to improve the skills in order to remain relevant and achieve desired goals.

Section 4:

GREATNESS BITES

George Washington Carver

George Washington Carver was born into slavery in Diamond, Missouri, around 1864. George Washington Carver had a vision to help himself and other farmers out of poverty which led him to create over a hundred things from the peanut.(He identified a **burden** that he was passionate about) Carver pioneered a mobile classroom to bring his lessons to farmers. The classroom was known as a "Jesup wagon," after New York financier and Tuskegee donor Morris Ketchum Jesup. Carver's work at Tuskegee included groundbreaking research on plant biology that brought him to national prominence. Many of these early experiments focused on the development of new uses for crops such as peanuts, sweet potatoes, soybeans and pecans. The hundreds of products he invented included plastics, paints, dyes and even a kind of gasoline.

Bites from the life of George Carver

- Your experiences and burdens could be an indicator of your purpose.
- You must decide to take steps to become great irrespective of your situation.
- Many people's lives are tied to your purpose; your decision to become great will help a lot of people.
- Your purpose makes you a creative person.

Section 5

<u>REFLECTIONS</u>

Now the LORD had said to Abram, Get you out of your country, and from your kindred, and from your father's house, to a land that I will show you: *And I will make of you a great nation, and I will bless you, and make your name great; and you shall be a blessing: And I will bless them that bless you, and curse him that curses you: and in you shall all families of the earth be blessed.*

GENESIS 12:1-3

❖Have you asked God what your location of greatness is?

❖Do you believe that God has allocated a place of greatness for you?

❖Do you believe your plans for your life are too small compared to what God has in store for you?

❖Do you know that God hears you when you speak?

❖ Abraham received God`s promises to go to his location of blessing.

- ❖ Are you confidence in God`s will for your life?
- ❖ Do some research of people that have excelled in your areas of interest? Read books, journals and articles that speak about your passions.

Chapter 2

FOCUSING THE ARROWS OF THE COMPASS

You are not here merely to make a living. You are here in order to enable the world to live more amply with greater vision, with a finer spirit of hope and achievement. You are here to enrich the world and you impoverish yourself if you forget the errand.

Woodrow Wilson

Section 1: The Arrow of the compass

In the previous chapter, it was established that a location is being sought after. So how do we focus the arrows of the compass to search for this particular location of greatness? Every human being is endowed with unique gifts, skills, talents and abilities to use as tools to become a blessing to humanity. These gifts or talents are sometimes the arrows of the compass that point us to our own destination.

One of the most celebrated writers of this generation, Chimamanda Ngozi Adichie, started her journey in Nigeria where she attended two years of medical school before she relocated. While in medical school, she edited The Compass, a magazine run by the university's Catholic medical students. At the age of 19, Adichie left Nigeria and moved to the United States for college. She studied communications and political science at Drexel University in Philadelphia and continued to pursue a master's degree in creative writing and African studies from Yale University and Johns Hopkins University. Since then she has received several awards and is now a sought-after international speaker. The arrows of her compass pointed her to creative writing and African studies, today she is lethal with her pen and her spoken words provoke the audience to deep thoughts and an array of emotions.

Certain professions like law, medicine, pharmacy, business and engineering are glorified in Nigeria and most parents encourage or even coerce their children into them. It is presumed that the smartest children are predestined to become physicians while students pursing degrees in the arts were not as intelligent. If Chimamanda had pursed medicine, I doubt if the world would have recognized her skills as a surgeon or a family care practitioner. She might have made a lot of money, but she would have felt unfulfilled because the arrows of her compass were pointing north while she was located west!

Another physician I had the privilege of knowing could have become a great lawyer or a politician early in life because of his extraordinary gift of the gab! In medical school, he was elected to lead the class and served in several political offices, defending the rights of the students, this individual deeply aspires to become a global leader or a political figure. When asked why he pursued a medical degree, the response was "When I was seven years old, a teacher asked all the students what they wanted to become and I said a physician, she laughed and said 'You can never become a doctor, I then took this as a challenge to become the physician that my teacher said I would never become." This physician worked in a hospital setting for a few years and disliked it; as a result, he now pursues a political path with hopes of becoming a political figure in the near future. I always wondered what heights this individual could have attained earlier in life if he was positioned appropriately, instead of being motivated by the desire to prove something to someone who was insignificant to his destiny.

The big question is, "Where is my arrow pointing and why am I focused on that location?" It is very important to understand the reason you are interested in what you are doing.

NOTE: When a person is positioned in their location of greatness, money is not a motivating force. For example: Medical student, Chiamanda, edited newspapers for free and the physician worked in several political offices to represent his fellow classmates voluntarily. People are naturally drawn to their areas of passion; however, many great men will attest that those passions were only building blocks upon which the foundation will be laid. To build a house, one must draw the plan and determine the end which is called vision.

Vision is what helps an individual focus the arrows of a compass when seeking the location of greatness, it can be described as the ability to see the finished mansion before you lay the first block of cement. Vision must be prayerfully sought out, no other person knows the end of one`s life better than the creator.

We don't know enough about the future to not consult the creator about the present.

Section 2

Stabilizing the arrow of the compass

To stabilize the arrow of the compass, one must understand who they are and why they possess those specific unique attributes. This requires focusing intentionally on understanding one's gifts, talents and experiences to see how it can be utilized for one's purpose. We are wired intentionally for a purpose. God put in us everything we need to fulfill a particular task and assignment.

For example, eagles are large powerfully built birds with heavy heads and large beaks. Their eyes are extremely powerful and is 3.6 times stronger in acuity than the eye of a human which enables them to spot potential prey from a very long distance. This keen eyesight is primarily attributed to their extremely large pupils which ensures minimal diffraction (scattering) of the incoming light. Most eagles grab their prey without landing and take flight with it so the prey can be carried to a perch and torn apart.

An eagle will never surrender to the size or strength of its prey. It will always give a fight to win its prey or regain its territory. Eagles can fly up to an altitude of 10,000 feet, but they are able to swiftly land on the ground. At 10, 000 feet, you will never find another bird. If you find another bird, it will mostly likely be the eagle.

At the age of 30, its physical body condition deteriorates fast making it difficult for it to survive. What is really interesting is that the eagle never gives up living. Instead it retreats to a mountaintop and over a five month period goes through a metamorphosis. It knocks off its own beak by banging it against a rock, plucks out its talons and then feathers. At every stage they produce a regrowth of the removed body parts, allowing the eagle to live for another 30 - 40 years.

An eagle may resemble a vulture in build and flight characteristics but has a fully feathered (often crested) head and strong feet equipped with great curved talons. One thing that differentiates the eagles from other birds is in foraging habits: eagles subsist mainly on live prey. They are too ponderous for effective aerial pursuit but try to surprise and overwhelm their prey on the ground. Like owls, many decapitate their kills. Because of their unusual strength, eagles have been a symbol of war and imperial power since Babylonian times.

Eagles are monogamous. They mate for life and use the same nest each year. They tend to nest in inaccessible places, incubating a small clutch of eggs for six to eight weeks. Their young mature slowly, reaching adult plumage in the third or fourth year. Physically, the eagle is wired for its particular purpose and assignment. Its physical characteristics equip it to catch its live prey, most birds don't not have the agility of the eagle, the eagle was wired to effectively to catch its prey. So why will God equip an eagle and not equip you to fulfill your assignment?

Currently, I am an occupational therapist by training, a speaker, entrepreneur and an author. When I look at my life, it is clear that I had been equipped for those assignments which are indicators of my purpose. Some of my natural abilities include public speaking, networking, compassionate service and building relationships. I also enjoy reading books, figuring out ways to solve problems for people, business minded and interceding for people in the place of prayer. Today, it is clear that I have been wired to fulfill an assignment in leadership with the focus on equipping people to maximize their potentials through knowledge, social entrepeneurship, service and prayer. Your abilities are indicators of your assignment.

You are wired for the problem you are created to solve

In every person lies the tools to become who God has called them to become. We have been equipped with the tools to do God's work. You have every potential (tapped and untapped) to carry out your assignment but you have to identify your gifts intentionally. A personal inventory checklist will help one identify what is inside of them. (See Workbook section for personal Inventory checklist table), this checklist will help one create an awareness of the gifting that the person has.

Personal Inventory Checklist **You have been wired for an assignment. Let`s take inventory of your gifts, interests, talents and aspirations.**		
Academic Interests	Talents	Hobbies

Section 3
Positioning the compass in the right location

When the compass is positioned in the right location, it becomes a tool that is effective to carry out an assignment, which is to give direction. Our lives are positioned as tools to carry out specific assignments. ***We are his workmanship created in him to do the good works which he has predestined for us. Ephesians 2:10***

A workman uses his tools for specific purposes because it has the ability to carry out the task. For example, a barber will always have a clipper in his possession because that is what is needed to cut hair. If the barber brought a spear to work, it will be ineffective in cutting hair, but will instead be useful to a hunter.

Individuals are tools positioned to carry out specific assignments.

To identify the right location where you are supposed to be a tool, these questions listed below will help you understand what is in you. This activity is also called **Compass Trails** in the workbook section

<u>Questions</u>

Passions

- What arouses you?
- What Triggers emotions in you?

Affection

- What are the things you don't need motivation to do?
- What do you like to do?
- What gives you joy when you do it?

Burdens

- ❖ What problems do you want to solve?
- ❖ What bothers you?
- ❖ What makes you mad?

Revelation

- ❖ What pictures, instructions or words has God shown you?
- ❖ What dreams are you having about the future?
- ❖ What do people notice about your abilities?

Potentials

- ❖ What are your gifts and talents?

Wisdom

- ❖ What areas do you possess deep insight in?

Family identity

- What trends do you see success in your family background?

Experience

- What positive or negative events shape your life?

As you answer these questions, you want to journal and pay attention to what comes to your mind as you are reading.

P.s: Our thoughts are inspired by God so we should take them very seriously.

Section 4:
GREATNESS BITES

If you begin to realize every moment in your life happened for the greater good of who you are, you can use it for others. It can really elevate you and change your whole trajectory. I think that is what happened to me. **TYLER PERRY**

Tyler Perry was born in New Orleans, Louisiana and experienced several difficulties in his life including physical and sexual abuse, financial hardships, homelessness and many other circumstances. However today he is an American actor, director, screenwriter, producer, author, and songwriter, fondly known for his character "Madea."

After watching an episode of Oprah Winfrey's talk show, he realized that one's difficult experiences could lead to personal breakthroughs. This then led him to begin a series of letters to himself, which became the basis for his musical, 'I Know I've Been Changed,' which tackled a lot of his own personal experiences such as child abuse. His letters also touched on forgiveness; a theme that has still remained central in many of his works reflecting a deep connection to his Christian faith. After saving $12,000, Perry's show debuted, which he directed, produced, and starred in at an Atlanta theater in 1992. Although this show was unsuccessful, he did not lose sight of his vision.

In 1998, his breakthrough came when he began to sell out shows. By 2013 he was worth millions of dollars and one of the wealthiest of African Americans. When asked how he made it through those obstacles, he proclaimed that his confidence in God's will and his vision have been a driving force. Today, his plays carry strong messages about the plan of God, faith, forgiveness and hope. God can write anyone's story… Tyler is a great man.

<u>BITES FROM TYLER PERRY`S LIFE</u>

- Your experiences are sometimes indicators of the problems you are supposed to solve.
- Your greatest pain might be God's tool to show your purpose.
- The will of God is stronger than the plan of the enemy.
- In spite of the failures, let your vision propel your destiny.
- Without hard work, it is impossible to build anything that is tangible.

Section 5:
Action Points

- Fill out the personal inventory checklist
- Identify your areas of interest
- Read about people who have similar interests
- Honestly write down where you are today and what you want to accomplish in five years.
- I commit to spending time with God to clarify the vision.
- I will read a book a month about my area of vision.
- I will partner with groups and individuals with similar mindsets.

REFLECTIONS

And the spirit of the LORD shall rest upon him, the spirit of wisdom and understanding, the spirit of counsel and might, the spirit of knowledge and of the fear of the LORD; And shall make him of quick understanding in the fear of the LORD: and he shall not judge after the sight of his eyes, neither reprove after the hearing of his ears.

ISAIAH 11:2-5

- What is my motivating force for the desire of my heart?
- What fuels my passion and where is my energy directed daily?
- Am I actively looking for my land of location or do I move

by following trends and patterns?

- What do I spend most of my time doing now?

Chapter 3

ZOOMING IN ON THE LOCATION

The hand of the LORD was upon me, and he brought me out by the Spirit of the LORD and set me in the middle of a valley; it was full of bones. He led me back and forth among them, and I saw a great many bones on the floor of the valley, bones that were very dry.

EZEKIEL 37:1-2

Section 1

Cardinal direction

A compass has four cardinal directions and serves as a navigational instrument, showing directions in a frame of reference relative to the surface of the earth. When the compass is in use, the rose is aligned with the real directions in the frame of reference pointing in any of the cardinal directions which are north, east, south and west. When followed, the instructions given will lead a person to the desired location. This same concept can be applied to our lives. Innate in us are gifts, skills, abilities, and passions that guide our decisions and make us gravitate toward certain areas of our lives.

The rose of the compass can be used to zoom in on a location. For example, someone destined to become a world class doctor feels a natural tendency to help people who are ill, or is attracted to solving medical problems. When an individual feels a natural attraction to a specific location, which could be a career like medicine, marketing, law, etc., a personal SWOT analysis can be conducted to examine the possibilities.

- S- Strengths
- W- Weakness
- O- Opportunities
- T- Threats

An understanding of a person`s strengths, weaknesses, threats and opportunities can be used as an indicator to determine one's cardinal direction. This will help a person begin to identify areas of life that a person has been wired for. In the workbook there are two temperament and personality tables that shows different aspects of a person`s character and attributes associated with different temperaments. One of the assesements also helps identify possible niches, or potiental career interests, which can be used as a guide. The closer a person draws to God, the more a person understand who they were created to be, this assesments can be tools to guide and understand what giftings and abilities are in a person and ultimately take stock introspectively of possible areas.

Section 2
Direction & Vision

Direction gives birth to a vision. When one identifies his direction, it is much easier to see the bigger picture. Everyone on the earth has specific assignments they are supposed to fulfill. When one spends time with God through reading the word, prayer, mediation and worship, those areas will be revealed. God will not come down and shout "Do this!" but will drop ideas and insights in one`s mind that can clarify the direction. Sometimes, God speaks through people so we must be sensitive to things that get or draw your attention.

Before I began writing n the year 2010, I was praying about my purpose and then one day I felt a strong urge within me to begin writing but quite frankly I did not know what to write about. I began to search my self to identify issues that bothered me and I realized that I hate to see people in hopeless situations, poverty or any kind of addictions. During that period, I used to lead worship at church, but one day I had a dream that I needed to go and start working with the homeless population so I ventured out to that area. It was while working with the group that I began to notice a trend of lack of purpose, that message resonated with me for a while. I then began my research about the topic and now today I speak about this topic to different groups and organize programs about it.

When the vision has not been defined, it is very important to continue to serve and not remain idle. As you begin to faithfully pursue your vision or that which you believe you are called to do, God begins to release the grace and anointing to do more, and will ultimately realign you to the right path. Sometimes your experiences make up the rose of your compass which will direct you to the right location. For example, Tyler Perry discovered that forgiveness and faith in God's will were the tools he needed to overcome his negative childhood experiences. These tools have become a central theme in his movies and have prospered him tremendously. Timing is everything, in 1992, Tyler Perry was not able to sell out any shows, but in 1998 he sold out the same shows that had previously failed. There is a set time of favor! When the right time for every purpose arrives, individuals will function at a more potent capacity. God gave Moses an assignment to deliver the children of Israel from oppression from the Egyptians. However, there was a set time for him to accomplish the task, Moses was an example of how a premature timing can cause one to act out of purpose. His assignment made him very angry and he killed the Egyptian in the wrong season which had consequences that delayed his purpose.

Vision is the ability to see the future and to determine its end point. Direction gives birth to vision; it brings one to a location of impact. As one walks in the direction of his vision, his five senses are activated to fulfill that assignment.

Vision is also faith in action. It's the ability to create things that have never existed. You must speak the things that you envision regularly because there is life in your words. Your voice is one the most powerful components of your vision. There is a location that is waiting for your voice. Unless you use your prophetic voice to call those things forth, they remain dead. That location is waiting for you to call things forth that have never existed. More potent power is released to you as you discover and begin to carry out God's assignment for your life in that area. This power allows a person to begin to operate efficiently in the direction of his vision.

The role of the holyspirit cannot be overemphazised on this journey. Two Biblical scrpitures have being my anthem when it comes to working in my purpose and depending on the help of the God the verses are as follows "He that God has sent, speaks the word of God and has been given the spirit without measure (John 3:34)" and "There is a spirit in man, the breath of the almighty God that gives him understanding (Job 32:8)".

A full understanding of one's direction can only be inspired by God. This could be through strong impressions placed on one's heart in the form of an inner voice, or through a prophetic voice by a pastor or a mentor. The Holy Spirit is the guide God has placed within us, to lead us in the way that we should go. HE knows the end from the beginning and shows us the steps to take to get there. The Bible says, "You will hear a voice behind you saying this is the way, walk in it." When we yield our lives to the order of the Holy

Spirit, HE shows us how to arrive at our location and enables us to call forth things into existence.

Thus, the Holy Spirit is the rose of the compass in our lives that leads us to our right location.

Section 3

Mapping out the Vision of Greatness

A map is a visual representation that shows all or part of the Earth's surface with geographic features, urban areas, roads, and other details. Mapping out the vision means to analyze the details of a journey and choose how to navigate to the desired location. Greatness is intentional, progressive and strategic. The details of a journey can be mapped out by setting goals. Goals should be broken down into actionable points to fulfill an assignment.

Ten key goal setting principles states:

1. Identify a major goal that is important to you. This goal must be specific, measurable and quantified.

2. Choose an exact date to accomplish tasks

3. Think of how to explore the goals in various ways and how to achieve them.

4. Decide upon a detailed action plan to follow, which will include steps to acquire knowledge, develop skills and build a team.

5. Compile a list of possible obstacles you have to overcome in order to reach your chosen goal or destination.

6. List the major benefits you will receive upon reaching these goals.

7. Form a master plan by writing down your answers to the previous six points.

8. Read your master plan aloud daily, once in the morning and at night until you achieve your goals.

9. Visualize yourself achieving this goal? How will you feel when it is achieved? What will it look like?

10. Start from where you are, don't wait for a perfect condition.

(Culled and modified from Goal setting, 13 secrets by World achievers)

A map will lead a person on a definite destination and will keep one focused on the steps to get there notwithstanding the diverse obstacles that can merge. You must never focus on the consequence of not getting to the destination, but rather focus on what you want to achieve, accomplish and receive.

Section 4:
GREATNESS BITES

The living God is our sufficiency. I have trusted Him for one dollar, I have trusted Him for thousands, and never trusted in vain. 'Blessed is the man that trusteth in Him'" (Ps. 34:8)

George Muller

He was the founder of the Ashley Down Orphanage, Bristol, England. Mr. Muller was born in Prussia, September 17, 1805. As a young person he lived a godless life, but at the age of twenty-one he made a decision with this statement saying "My whole life shall be one service for the living God. He never asked help from anyone and never hinted that help was needed. Solely in answer to believing prayer, he received more than one and a half million sterling, ($7,500,000) for the building and maintenance of

"God's Orphanage," for his missionary enterprises, and for the circulation of the Scriptures.

He has made tremenodous impact, his homes houses ten thousand destitute orphans who have been received, trained, educated, and sent out into the world.

In his old age, he traveled nearly two hundred thousand miles in forty-two countries, preaching the Gospel to three millions of hearers.

He died at the age of ninety-three. He was a great man.

Bites from the life of Muller

- He lived a life of service.
- He made a decision to be great.
- His faith in God's provision was remarkable and brought forth great gains.
- His life empowered the helplessness of the orphans.

Section 5

Action points

- Make a decision to live a life of service
- Think of ways you can utilize your current profession to reach out to people in need
- Start praying to God to reveal the areas you can use to impact your generation positively
- Start with where you are.

REFLECTIONS

The hand of the LORD was upon me,
and he brought me out by the Spirit of the LORD
and set me in the middle of a valley; it was full of bones.
He led me back and forth among them,
and I saw a great many bones
on the floor of the valley, bones that were very dry.
EZEKIEL 37:1-2

- How has God led you in the past?
- Where does the spirit of lord lead you?
- The problems that you see around you, the dry bones are they the problems you are supposed to solve?
- If you ever imagined an ideal life, what will it be?
- How different is your ideal life from the life you have now?

Chapter 4

Laying Blocks on the Location

When we have done all we can do, Remarkable things happen when we surrender.

DEBBIE FORD

Section 1:

Strategizing the Vision

Strategy is defined as the steps to carry out a vision. As defined earlier, vision is the ability to see the future; mission is how you impact the future; and strategy is the ladder between the vision and the mission.

After goals are set, definite strategies must be put in place. For example, a goal and strategy can be

Goal: I want to raise 2,000 to fund my magazine start up in 3 months.

Strategy: 1. I will create online fund raisers,

2. I will work extra hours at work,

3. I will baby sit twice a week and save the money. Strategies are definite ways of accomplishing a task. Great strategies are inspired by God in the place of meditation and quietness. There are three parts that make up a human being; our spirit, soul and body. It is

very important to align all three aspects of our being towards our desired vision. The soul houses our emotions, personalities and things that make us who we are. Our spirit is what gives us the ability to relate with God while our body follows the most potent desires within our spirit and soul. Without a definite purpose within all three aspects of our being, we will not fully express our desired purpose and therefore cannot fully acquire the strategies we need. There must be a harmony within all three aspects of our being to align with what we are expecting to achieve because, we will birth into fruition the most innate desire of our heart.

The human spirit communicates with God and can be used to control the soul and body. The spirit man is led and empowered by God which allows man to commune with God and give birth to divine strategies. This revelation must be in the spirit man first, before the soul and body can align with it. To begin a strategy, you must align all parts of yourself to carry out our assignment. Strategy is an intentional plan carried out by working out actionable goals.

Section 2: Aligning with Builders of the structures

Every house is built by someone but the builder of all things is God. Having God as the ultimate builder requires having an intimate relationship with him where one can hear the voice of God to receive the pattern for building. The Holy Spirit is the first builder to align with, a man's spirit is led and empowered by God therefore He receives instruction to build great structures there. This revelation must be in the spirit man first, before the soul and body can align with it. So, if you are probably wondering what all this spirit talk means, you are not alone! For many years, I wondered until I began to surrender my authority and desires to God by spending more time reading his word, praising him and talking to Him like a friend. Soon I began to recognize his presence, the still small voice and the aura of his glory. The more I read the Bible, I was able to discern between what he has done through men in the past, and what he wants me to know. This led me to begin to pray that Isaiah 11:1-4 become a reality in my own life.

And the spirit of the LORD shall rest upon him, the spirit of wisdom and understanding, the spirit of counsel and might, the spirit of knowledge and of the fear of the LORD; and shall make him of quick understanding in the fear of the LORD: and he shall not judge after the sight

of his eyes, neither reprove after the hearing of his ears: But with righteousness shall he judge the poor, and reprove with equity for the meek of the earth: and he shall smite the earth: with the rod of his mouth, and with the breath of his lips shall he slay the wicked.

It is very important to depend on the leading of the spirit for quick understanding and a discerning spirit to not judge after the eyes or the hearing of the ears but to depend on the spirit of God for wisdom, knowledge and counsel. Beautiful and glorious things are not seen, they are perceived with the eyes of the spirit. Man cannot fully discern his journey because he does not know enough about the future to make good decisions. A man's spirit must be in constant communication with God to relate with him as a son. Sin quenches the glory of God in a man. It distorts one's ability to hear from God. Even though sin might not cancel what God has purposed for a man, it affects one's ability to relate and understand God's purpose. To maximize purpose and zoom in accurately on how to build, one must desire to receive the Holy Spirit because He (GOD) is the ultimate guide and gives power to do work.

Every person is distinct with different personality types, strengths, weaknesses, passions and abilities which form the basis of who we are. The Holy Spirit can change or groom aspects of our lives to fit our purpose. For example, He can inspire a quiet natured person to become an excellent orator because he has ordained him to preach the gospel. We must master our personalities to identify areas of weakness as well as strength. Some tests like the personality tests in the workbook can help an individual understand his personality which can be strong indicators to help streamline areas of passions. One must actively seek God continually by spending time in fellowship with Him and in His word. Then, and only then, can one fully understand what God, the builder is saying. God will clarify the vision of a man by showing him the end from the beginning. Aligning with builders means to find help or relevant resources to erect a structure. This could include building a team, finding people whose vision complement and are aligned towards the same direction as yours.

Section 3

Building in the right location.

Have you ever observed that as big trees grow they provide shed and nutrients for other smaller trees? This is what happens to a life in the right location. At the right location, a person is positioned to be a blessing to others as they fully express their gifts, natural abilities and passions. This location could be a career, idea, city, family and otherwise. In Genesis 1:28, God blessed man and commanded him to be fruitful, multiply, replenish the earth, subdue it, and have dominion over all living things that move on the earth. When a life is positioned in the right location, He fulfills the five commands: fruitfulness, multiplication, replication, subduing and dominating

God, the creator of the whole world, knows about every subject under the heaven. He is the one that can reveal secrets and mysteries to a man about how to operate and fulfill these commands in the right location. He who God has sent speaks the words of God and He has put His spirit in him without limit. (JOHN 3:34) When a man is at the right location, he goes forth as one sent by God and then speaks revolutionary insights and wisdom, as inspired by the spirit of God, to bring change to that location. As previously stated, a great tree is characterized by its ability to bear fruit, provide shade and nutrients for smaller trees, and withstand pressure from environmental forces. Smaller trees are limited by their ability to produce based on the surface areas they occupy. When a person does not seek to discover his purpose or land of location, he is limited in his level of impact and slowly withers away.

Greatness is not about attaining wealth, resources, status or a grandiose state. However, it is a position of service and impact. Great people are problem solvers, change agents, solution deliverers who add value to their world, and their status becomes dependent on the magnitude of the problems they can solve. Joseph and Daniel, in the Bible, were promoted to great levels of authority because they were able to solve problems that troubled the rulers of the land. They both acknowledged God as the one who reveals wisdom to solve problem. Another great example was David. He removed the armor given to him to fight Goliath, took his simple sling and a stone and located the head of Goliath as he released it through faith in God. I believe that God's strength was added as David stepped out and threw that stone, which knocked down the head of Goliath. When a person is positioned in the right location, God releases great strength and authority to solve problems that kill the giants on the land as he steps out in faith. As a tree grows in the right location, weeds will always try to compete with the growth of the seed. Sin and evil communication are the weeds that can compete with the growth of a destiny . . . Run from it! Evaluate the relationships around you if they have the same values, because we pull strength from the people we communicate with on a regular basis. Two people on two different frequencies will either pull down or displace the person on a higher altitude. It is easier to be pulled down than to be pushed up. Evil communication corrupts good manners. Some things, or people, you have to run away from because they are obstacles to your destiny. They have been positioned to reel you away from your glorious destiny. Portiphar's wife was a trap, positioned to steal the destiny of Joseph. However, he secured his greatness when he ran leaving behind his garments in her hand.

You must determine today that you are divinely positioned for greatness, so choose today to leave whatever you have been holding onto that gives the devil access to your destiny and run upward! God has positioned helpers to walk the journey of greatness with you. Ask God to open your eyes to see clearly who they are and what roles they must play in your life.

Section 4

GREATNESS BITES

I believe the power to make money is a gift from God, he declared ... to be developed and used to the best of our ability for the good of mankind. **JOHN ROCKEFELLER**

John Rockefeller was born on July 8, 1839, in Richford, New York. As a young boy, he wished to get rich, but was heavily burdened. How he could do so and serve Jesus? This left him to spend the first half of his life pursuing money, following the guidance he had received as a boy from his father, a businessman: "Get money, get it honestly, and then give it wisely." Rockefeller, at 16, got a job as a clerk in Cleveland. A desire arose within him to become a great merchant as he looked through the windows at Lake Erie, loaded with merchandise from cargo ships. He soon co-founded Clark & Rockefeller, a shipping firm, specializing in the trading and transportation of grain and fresh fish on the Great Lakes. He attributed the success of the company to his imperial confidence in God's will, tithing religiously, working hard, leading, and organizing and his ability to look at columns of figures for 12 hours; attributes derived from the discipline and focus he learned from his mother.

Through hard work and tenacity, he soon created Standard Oil, which controlled virtually all U.S. oil production and comprised the greatest corporate empire the world had ever known. He spent the second half of his life involved in large-scale philanthropy, which focused on medical research and education. This led to the Rockefeller Institute for Medical Research in New York City, now known as the Rockefeller

University, which has been highly influential in medicine over the years and a home for many Nobel Prize winners. He also contributed immensely to the development of African Americans through education and other charitable ventures. He was often characterized for his faith in God and philanthropy. His works still live on after his death. He was a great man.

BITES FROM THE LIFE OF ROCKEFELLER

- He had a strong sense of identity.
- He had confidence in the will of the creator.
- He had a potent desire to discover how to use his gifts for the kingdom
- He was a hard worker.
- He had a sense of purpose.

Section 5

Action Points

- What is my motivating force for the desire of my heart?
- What fuels my passion and where is my energy directed daily?
- Complete the activities in the workbook to identify possible areas of passion.

- What kings need to be set up for me? Kings are mighty men that can use their influence for me.

- Write down areas where you need great men to help you and pray regularly that this destiny helpers find you.
- Write down areas where kings need to be removed so you can ascend in life.

- **Confession:** I confess that as I have been led by the spirit of God to my rightful location, I am here to build, uproot and plant. I attract help from the right people, people of influence, people of integrity, visionary minded people, God fearing and loving people are positioned to help me in my location. I pronounce a separation between myself and people who are destroyers, people set to oppose God`s plan for my life. I have been set apart for great works, nations are coming to my light and people that I have not known will serve and promote God`s work through me.

- Who do I spend most of my time with and how they help me fulfill God`s plan?

- Who do I need to align with? Who do I need to separate from?

- What habits in my life do I need to change that will hinder my growth?

- How do I set my self apart for God`s purpose?

Chapter 5

Building Great Structures on your land

Great men are they who see that the spiritual is stronger than material force, that thoughts rule the world.

RALPH WALDO EMERSON

Section 1:
Building: The process

After a long search for a destination, the first thing one does upon arrival is to place the luggage down. How does this refer to one's place of greatness and the process of building? When a person discovers their location of greatness, the land might be bare and empty. For some, it might be filled with precious treasures, and for others, they might have to cultivate the land to bear fruit. The life of Abraham will be used as a case study for building when one arrives at a place of purpose. By faith Abraham was called to go out into a place which he would later receive for an inheritance. He obeyed and went out, not knowing where he went.

By faith he sojourned in the land of promise, as in a strange country, dwelling in tabernacles with Isaac and Jacob, the heirs with him of the same promise: for he looked for a city which foundation is God.

<u>Key lessons In Abraham's life</u>

- Faith
- Obedience
- Sojourned in a strange land
- Looked for a city with a foundation whose maker is God.

Without faith, it is impossible to accept and build on your land of greatness. God might lead you to a land that looks like you are going to go through a setback but ultimately God has hidden treasures on the land if only you obey.

Faith can be likened to the wings of an eagle. Once opened, there are no limits to the altitude and speed in which that bird can take off.

Without faith, it is impossible to obey or please God because they that come to God must believe that he is real, and he is the rewarder of them who seek him.

There was a time in my life when I found myself in a hopeless situation. I was trying to progress with my career and all advancements, in terms of a higher education, were denied. During that period, I was working on a job that was beneath my qualification and all hope was lost. On a fateful Sunday service, I heard God say, *"Bring your last paycheck, all of it."* I was so scared that I did not know what to do, but somehow faith swelled up in my heart. So I cashed the check and took all the money to church as a seed offering. The following week God told me to send my application to a graduate program that had closed, I obeyed and that week someone dropped out of the program and I was given the admission. I also needed money to complete the course. God used helpers to give me scholarships and provide the resources to fund the rest of the bill. Is He a faithful God or what? That became my testimony; a reference point to have faith and believe God for tougher situations that came in the future.

To sojourn on the land means to reside on a land for a short period of time, typically on a destination somewhere else. On the journey to greatness, a person might find themselves in a place temporarily because there might be something, a person or an opportunity that is supposed to contribute to the person's destiny. This might result in a rearrangement or repositioning which could happen in the form of losing a job or circumstances beyond one's control. If the repositioning was orchestrated by God, it is a set up for greater things! *Deep valleys always precede great heights.* This quote speaks of the difficulties and challenges that could plague a person during a period of sojourning to the location. However, deep valleys are seasons of growth and preparation in a person's life to lead them to greater dimensions. In those seasons, seeming dark and deep, one must learn to have total trust in God, that he is able to lead one to the desired end. *"I know whom I have believed"* must be the watchword and it is evidence in how the person prepares to build a great structure on that land. God has to strip us of the old so we can receive the new. It is in this season that one will discover the foundation God has made, as one actively searches for it.

One of the ways to begin the building process in on your location of greatness is to make a covenant with God. A covenant is "a binding agreement or arrangement between two parties, whether unilaterally or bilaterally, involving obligations, responsibilities or obedience". When God makes a covenant with man, He is bound to the terms of the covenant and surely fulfills his promises.

As one steps into a land, it is very important to step down and declare the end from the beginning before placing one's luggage down.

You declare the end from the beginning through prayer, spoken words, training, building faith by hearing (messages, bible study) and actions. When building a physical house, the builders have to follow the architect's instructions and then the city council has to approve the conditions of the house before the house can be erected. The same rule can be applied to things in the spiritual realm, we are kings and priests made to reign and have dominion in every area of life. We have to offer our priestly duties before we can be ordained kings over any domain. To be a priest means to surrender our lives as living sacrifices and to get instructions from God on how to build great structures. A king must be well equipped with strategies, wisdom and authority to effectively carry out an assignment. Instructions to carry out an assignment are received as he carries out his priestly duties. *It is in the place of his priestly duties, that the mystery of God's will and purpose is fully revealed.* It is imperative to clarify the assignment first, before building on the land. A building is only as strong as its foundation, so be very careful what you attract during this period because cracks in a foundation show up when the weight of the building has increased. Every person is not your helper, and every open door is not meant for you to walk through, some people lost their lives because they were in the wrong place at the time or with the wrong people. You have to confirm with God to see who He has aligned to walk with you.

You don't know enough about your life to make important decisions without seeking God's direction.

No one knows enough about their future to make decisions without the direction of God. As many that are led by the spirit, they are the sons of God. If you have never received the gift of the Holy Spirit, you must pray for it. When Jesus left the earth, He said I will leave you a comforter, the Holy Spirit. He will teach you all things and bring all things to remembrance.

When a man does not depend on God for guidance, he has made himself a god. God's word says *"I am the lord your God, you shall have no other gods but me,"*

(Exodus 20:3) he also says *"I will lead you beside still waters (Psalms 23:2), I am the lord your*

God I am the one that teaches you to profit". (Isaiah 48:17)

No other voice should be louder than the voice of the Lord which can be through a deep impression on our hearts, dreams, visions, a still small voice and words that stick out to us as we read the bible; or spoken through prophets of God which you have received before.

Prophecies come to confirm to you what God has already told you. Prophecies come to edify you and if it does not do either of the aforementioned, you might want to take heed to what you hear. God speaks a meassage and many times confirms it to our hearing more than once. ***Once He has spoken, twice have we heard that all power belongs to God?***

Section 2

Cementing the structures with Vision

In the previous chapter, we established that your location might be bare and waiting for you to build on it. Building great structures is intentional and strategic. When David was building the temple, he relied on God for direction.

Then David gave to Solomon his son the pattern of the porch, and of the houses thereof, and of the treasuries thereof, and of the upper chambers thereof, and of the inner parlors thereof, and of the place of the mercy seat. And the pattern of all that he had by the spirit, of the courts of the house of the LORD, *and of all the chambers round about, of the treasuries of the house of God.* ***(1 Samuel 2:6)***

The emphasis is that David received from the Spirit of the Lord, the pattern to build great structures.

This gave him a vision and direction to know what to build.

As we receive direction from God about how to build our structures, we must remember that we are co-creators of our destiny and God expects us to intentionally develop the vision for the structures he has given us.

The frame of reference for building will be the acronym G.R.E.A.T, to establish and determine how every structure will be built.

G-Growth

R- Reasons

E-Energy

A-Acquire

T-Treasures

GROWTH

For a plant to grow, it starts from the root where it is dark and lonely. Growth is a process, it requires hard work, periods of pruning, failures and trials to introduce a person to their strengths, weaknesses and potentials. This dark season of growth reveals purpose to a person. This season also points out certain weaknesses in one's personalities needing to be addressed before a structure can stand firmly. Some very destructive points that can hinder a person include anger, greed, jealousy, bitterness, revenge, laziness, indiscipline, inappropriate sexual behaviors and desires, borrowing, arrogance and pride. Many men built great structures, but pulled them down because they failed to address these weak points. For growth to occur, we must consciously take intentional and deliberate actions to conquer the weaknesses or things that oppose growth in our lives. This can be compared to the larvae stage of a butterfly. This is the stage of an insect's life during which its final form is still hidden or masked. After the larvae stage metamorphosis takes place, it brings forth the final form of a beautiful butterfly, which is colorful and radiant. When a life allows itself to go through a growth stage, it becomes colorful, attractive and fruitful. The foundation of any great structure is very important, during this process objects must be cemented firmly in the ground to avoid cracks that can eventually lead to the breaking down of the whole structure.

REASONS

To build strong structures, reasons must be guided by a vision. Vision is the end product of every achievement. Without a vision, the reasons for building will change along the way, as the person encounters challenges. Before starting any structure, one must identify clearly the reasons for building. Is your purpose the reason why you are building? What other factors must be influencing your reasons? Is your reason externally or internally motivated? Is your reason strong enough to die for? What do you want to have accomplished after this great structure is built? As Christians whatever we do must be to glorify God. For a foundation to stand sure, God's purpose must be the motivating force, surely we cannot lie to God he knows our thoughts from away.

The foundation of God stands sure, having this seal, The Lord knows them that are his, and everyone who calls upon the name of the lord must depart from iniquity (2 TIM 2:19)

When the reason is according to His purpose to establish the earth, to exalt His house to the top of the mountain as a place where nations will run to, to inherit the desolate heritages for God, to bring light to dark places, then God, and all the resources in heaven, become committed to show forth the greatness of God through that person. This person then becomes unstoppable and whatever he does, yields great results. Another reason to build is because we are sent to light up dark places. The bible says that:

Have respect unto the covenant: for the dark places of the earth are full of the habitations of cruelty. (Psalms 74:20)

Dark places are places of obscurity, where lives are in bondage, injustice and poverty. God sends His vessels to bring light to dark places. As you build, let the dark places that you are supposed to lighten up, become the reason for your vision.

ENERGY

Every system needs some form of energy to function. One of Einstein's laws states that "Energy cannot be created nor destroyed but can be transferred from one form to another". When a television is not plugged in, its potential is untapped and it serves no purpose. However, when you plug it in to an electrical outlet and power it on, it becomes of great use to its owner. So, it is with our lives, when we are not plugged in to our creator, our potentials and purpose is untapped and is not fully expressed. But when we plug our lives to our creator, we become useful, powerful and able to perform work. God is light and in Him there is no darkness at all. We need to receive our energy from God to light up our location of greatness so we can function with the power to do work. We plug in through worship, mediating in his presence, spending time in his work and fellowshipping with other believers.

ACQUIRE

To acquire means to obtain something. After discovering one's purpose, one must acquire knowledge, helpers, strategy and resources to build a great structure. If the axe is dull, it will require more strength to cut down a tree, but skill and wisdom will make the task easier. Without knowledge, every dream and purpose is doomed! Knowledge gives a person insight, enhances creativity, productivity and vision, thus the cement of any great structure. Knowledge is to be sought after. It can be acquired through several sources. The first source is God. If any man lacks wisdom, he should seek his creator who can speak through ideas, thoughts, images and dreams. By wisdom, a house is built and by understanding, it is filled with precious things. Finding people that have similar interests, reading material, attending conferences and continually seeking out information in those areas will help understand how to maximize efforts in that location.

An African proverb says "You climb a tall tree by stepping on the shoulders of a tall person." Finding mentors and people who have thrived in similar areas of your purpose, will help gain speed on how to build a firm structure and make it very secure. The journey to fulfill purpose is easier with the right helpers. The Holy Spirit is the first helper. People who have traveled down similar paths are other forms of help. It is also very important for God to lead you to your shepherd, a pastor who has the heart of God, who will teach you principles and hold you accountable spiritually. One must acquire strategy to execute, before building. An architect draws a blue print structure before the project is executed. So, our lives must be drawn out before we go on a journey. You must then, put in place measurable goals to evaluate and re-evaluate our outcomes to maximize impact.

TREASURES

Treasures are valuable resources, which are of great importance to its owner. The gifts, abilities, talents, resources, pain and skills in a person are the treasures that enable a person to add value to their world. No two people are the same, each person has a different set of abilities, experiences, and passions that make them unique.

Think for a second, what do I like doing? What areas have I excelled effortlessly? What do I like to do naturally? What areas do ideas flow naturally to me? Write them down! This is a pointer to the treasures within. Treasures could be tangible and intangible. Some people will attract wealth and earthly treasures to finance the kingdom's assignments while others will use their skills, talents and services. A man's gift makes room for him and brings him before great men. The secrets of God are treasures to be desired which He reveals to His servants. When a man has access to information, his journey becomes easier and shorter. This should be a heartfelt desire and prayer, "Lord, show me your secrets especially about my life". The lasting treasures are the ones God gives a man, no earthly treasure can truly compare with this.

Section 3

Greatness

Seeds should grow to become great trees. Chicks should grow to become great birds and babies should grow up to be great people because God expects it. It is mandate!

God blessed man and said, "Be fruitful and increase in number; fill the earth, subdue and have dominion. Rule over the fish in the sea and the birds in the sky and over every living creature that moves on the ground." GENESIS 1:28.

The four characteristics of Greatness are:

1. Fruitfulness
2. To Subdue
3. Authority to rule
4. Dominion

When a person exhibits four of those characteristics, they come into a position of greatness. Discovering one's purpose and developing it will lead one to a position of greatness exhibiting those four characteristics. A great tree provides shades and nutrients for other smaller trees and yields fruit that others can benefit from. Greatness is God's plan for his children because he says we are priests and kings made to reign with him in heavenly places. We are priests first before we become kings. A priest spends time communing with God to inquire and offer sacrifices before delivering it to the people, which then gives his strategies and wisdom to rule as a king.

To rule as a king means to dominate a sphere of influence, to have authority and to be an influential figure. This can be through several platforms like a career, an industry, natural abilities and talents. Kings need wisdom and knowledge to rule effectively which can be acquired through prayer, books and avenues of mentorship. When we work in authority as great people, we exhibit the nature of our creator, a visible representation of an invisible God. We are meant to reproduce after our creator exhibiting his traits.

To be great means to become a problem solver, a solution to crisis, to bring answers to areas of long standing questions and to be positioned for impact.

Section 4

GREATNESS BITES

The Strength of a word from God

PASTOR JOSIAH AKINDAYOMI

Pastor Akindayomi is founder of the Redeemed Christian Church International, who was born into the

Akindayomi family of Ondo, State of Nigeria. The RCCI was founded in 1952 after hearing the voice within him saying, "You will be my servant." Pa Akindayomi never wanted to become a pastor, so he decided to ignore the voice and as a result experienced many failures hitherto before fully yielding to the grace of God. He then declared, "Lord, I will go wherever you want me to go" and thus asked for signs to confirm that this was indeed God's call.

Pa Akindayomi could neither read nor write the English language but the name of the church was revealed to him in a vision. He miraculously scribbled down the individual letters in English which, when put together, read "The Redeemed Christian Church of God." God also promised in that vision to take the church to the ends of the earth and declared that the Lord Jesus Christ would meet the church when he returned in glory. In the early 1970s, God had told him that his successor, who was not yet a member of the church, would be a young educated man and thus when a young university lecturer joined the church in 1973, Akindayomi was able to recognize him in the Spirit as the one whom the Lord had spoken of. This man, Enoch Adejare Adeboye, a lecturer in mathematics at the University of Lagos, soon became involved in the activities of the church. Today the church is thriving with over 2,000 parishes of the church in Nigeria alone.

Other African nations include: Côte d'Ivoire, Ghana, Zambia, Malawi, Zaire, Tanzania, Kenya, Uganda, Gambia, Cameroon, and South Africa. In Europe, the church has spread to England, Germany, and France. In the Americas, there are several parishes in almost every state and in several provinces in Canada.

One prominent program of the church is the Holy Ghost service, an all-night miracle service, held on the first Friday of every month at the Redemption camp, which averages about 500,000 people. The church is still thriving on the strength of God's word.

BITES FROM THE LIFE OF PA AKINDAYOMI

- He received a promise from God.
- He yielded to God's leading.
- God directed him about whom to pick as a successor.
- God never goes back on His covenant.
- The word of the Lord, in his life, has been a blessing to millions of people on the earth, even after his death.

Section 5

Action points

- What strategies have I put in place to grow in wisdom?
- What sacrifices must I start making to ensure my growth?
- Can God trust me to be the ruler He can trust?
- How have I been foolish in the past?
- A great book that I recommend is, "The Seven Mountains of Prophecy". It talks about the roles of believers in the last days.

Chapter 6

WHY MUST I BECOME GREAT?

It is a mandate from God; "Verily, verily, I say unto you, He that believeth on me, the works that I do shall he do also; and greater works than these shall he do; because I go unto my Father.

JOHN 14:12

Section 1: Positioned at the top of the mountain

In recent times, we have seen different sectors of the world crumble; the financial sector, housing and others have crumbled. Natural disasters, wars and instabilities are the order of the day around the world. Many people are looking for answers as they have questions that cannot be answered. As we approach the last days God wants to position people as tools in high places of greatness to represent him. He wants to raise people to take up different sectors in the world and give them wisdom that will solve problems, which will ultimately lead people back to him. This can only be achieved when people seek the purpose for which they were created. It is in that place of destiny that God has allocated for each man that He will receive the wisdom to rule.

Another of the reasons why we must aspire for greatness is to fulfill a prophetic mandate as Isaiah 2:2 says; *"And it shall come to pass in the last days, that the mountain of the Lord's house shall be established in the top of the mountains, and shall be exalted above the hills; and all nations shall flow to it. And many people shall go and say, come you, and let us go up to the mountain of the LORD, to the house of the God of Jacob; and he will teach us of his ways, and we will walk in his paths: for out of Zion shall go forth the law and the word of the LORD from Jerusalem."*

God wants to raise people who are solution providers, wise builders who are dependent on him for divine wisdom to solve problems. This people are positioned as an army fighting without physical weapons but equipped with strategies to build, restore, plant and uproot systems in the world, they are positioned in different sectors of life, highly revelant and spiritual, they are professionals in the marketplace, government house, hospitals, schools, social and public working in their purpose. They are dependent on the strong hand of God to provide them with solutions to solve problems ultimately bringing people back to knowing him. That is why we must seek to discover and develop our purpose so we can be effective tools in God`s hand.

Greatness is a state of dependency on the strong hand of God. No one will make a truly lasting impact without the wisdom and direction of God as the propeller to do great things. This requires wisdom and anointing that can only come from people who have eyes that see beyond the situations, and ears to hear what God is saying for each season.

Solomon was a perfect example of someone who received wisdom for greatness. *"And all Israel heard of the judgment which the king had judged; and they feared the king: for they saw that the wisdom of God was in him, to do justice."*

1 KINGS 3:28

He had the wisdom to discern what to do. Every great man must ask for this level of wisdom to know what to do.

Section 2
Reward of Greatness

Another reason why God will want to raise great men in these times is to rebuild fallen and destroyed sectors. This man must have the foresight of Nehemiah, as renovators and restorers, to bring back the glory of God.

Then I said to them, "You see the trouble we are in: Jerusalem lies in ruins, and its gates have been burned with fire. Come, let us rebuild the wall of Jerusalem, and we will no longer be in disgrace." I also told them about the gracious hand of my God on me and what the king had said to me. They replied, "Let us start rebuilding." So, they began this good work. **NEHEMIAH 2:17**

God needs a man who will arise as a rebuilder of sectors, so the name of God will be exalted as the only source of solution, where all nations run to for refuge and help.

As we know, the anointing flows from the top down. God wants to raise men who will carry Daniel's anointing for government, as they depend on God to reveal secrets to them.

The king answered to Daniel, and said, of a truth it is, that your God is a God of gods, and a Lord of kings, and a revealer of secrets, seeing you could reveal this secret. Then the king made Daniel a great man, and gave him many great gifts, and made him ruler over the whole province of Babylon and chief of the governors over all the wise men of Babylon. **DANIEL 2:47** Men who depend on God for direction are needed in high places to lead this world back to the creator as the solution provider.

The end point of greatness must not be that a man will be exalted or recognized for his great accomplishments, but that the greatness of God will be shown through him.

God is also interested in raising great men who will ask for the anointing of Abraham to receive new territories and intergenerational covenant blessings so that the world will know that it is the Lord who gives men power to get wealth. He took him outside and said,

"Look up at the sky and count the stars—if indeed you can count them." Then he said to him, "So shall your offspring be." Abram believed the LORD and he credited it to him as righteousness. He also said to him, "I am the LORD, who brought you out of Ur of the Chaldeans to give you this land to take possession of it." **GENESIS 15:5-7**

He wants men who operate at levels to understand that faith and trust in God is the way to be lifted in life, and that as many men who covenant with Him, God can deliver His promise. **Great men must be people of worship who must continually** stay **in His presence.** Worship is what God requires from every man. A person of worship carries God's presence around with him because he dwells in worship. Great men must also covenant with God to propagate the kingdom agenda as His ambassadors.

Section 3

Utilizing your talents

Another reason why we must be great is because to whom much is given, much is required. Like the proverb of the talents, God has given each man talents according to his ability.

A man called his servants and entrusted his wealth to them, to one he gave five bags of gold, to another two bags, and to another one bag, each according to his ability. The man who had received five bags of gold went at once and put his money to work and gained five bags more. So also, the one with two bags of gold gained two more but the man who had received one bag went off, dug a hole in the ground and hid his master's money. When the master returned he took away the talent from the one who had only one talent and 'you wicked, lazy servant! So you knew that I harvest where I have not sown and gather where I have not scattered seed? "'So he took the bag of gold from him and gives it to the one who has ten bags for whoever has will be given more, and they will have abundance. Whoever does not have, even what they have will be taken from them. And throw that worthless servant outside, into the darkness, where there will be weeping and gnashing of teeth.

MATTHEW 25:14-30

To the man who refuses to use his talents to become great for God, the ability he has will be taken from him and given to another who has discovered his purpose and is using it to make a difference. Is purpose really my map to greatness? Yes it is. Discover your purpose and it will become a guide that will lead you to your greatness! Your land of location is waiting for you to fill it with great treasures. God is waiting to make you a great ambassador for Him. What are you doing about it? He wants to use your talents that he gave you to make you great for Him! Start now! The world is dark and it is awaiting your light to shine.

For the dark places are filled with the habitations of wickedness.

PSALM 74:20

Your purpose will bring light to dark places. There are people who will remain in bondage until you begin to walk in your purpose. You have been sent forth as a deliverer to your generation. Don't disappoint God!

Your purpose is the map that leads you to greatness!

Section 4

GREATNESS BITES

Yet even in earthly matters I believe that 'the invisible things of Him from the creation of the world are clearly seen, being understood by the things that are made, even His eternal power and Godhead'; and I have never seen anything incompatible between those things of man which can be known by the spirit of man which is within him and those higher things concerning his future, which he cannot know by that spirit.

MICHAEL FARADAY

One of the greatest scientists of all times known for his tremendous contributions to science, Michael Faraday was an English chemist and physicist known for his work on the connectivity of electricity and magnetism. He was the first scientist to convert mechanical energy into electric energy, which was a crucial step towards development of the electric motor and generator. He was known for his unusual character and his faith in God.

In his scientific studies, he sought to understand the beauty, symmetry, and organization of God's creation. He, like Job in the Bible, acknowledged that a man cannot find God by his own reasoning and relied on the Scriptures alone to reveal Him.

Faraday wrote that a Christian finds his guide in the word of God, and commits the keeping of his soul into the hands of God. He boldly declared that assurance of everything comes from the word of God, and if his mind was troubled by the cares and fears, which assail him, he can go nowhere but in prayer to the throne of grace and to Scripture. He deeply relied on the wisdom of God and was known for his deep sense of humility.

BITES FROM THE LIFE OF FARADAY

- No matter the great heights he attained, he remained humble.
- His vision was to understand the beauty, symmetry, and organization of God's creation in his scientific studies.
- He relied on the word of God for wisdom.
- His relationship with God was his guiding light and force.
- He worked hard on his project to become the best.

Section 5:
ACTION POINTS

Confession: Greatness is God's plan for my life. I am created for greatness and will show forth the greatness of Christ. I am created to bring forth a new dimension of heaven to earth. I am a part of God's covenant to establish the earth. I decree that favor, success, helpers, grace, and mercy locates me today. No plan of the devil will come to pass in my life. I declare that I have integrity, character, and skill. I am righteous and no evil work will be found with me. None of God's good promises for my life will fail, instead I will grow in intimacy with my Father and He will lead me to my greatness in Jesus' name. I am a light to my world and I now operate at my maximum capacity in Jesus' name. Amen.

- o Commit to joining an organization that is already working in that capacity.
- o Commit to reading professional journals and books about your sector.
- o Develop a daily prayer and word life.
- o Seek God to reveal secrets about your purpose to you.

Chapter 7

GREATNESS IS INTENTIONAL

"Keep your dreams alive. Understand to achieve anything requires faith and belief in yourself, vision, hard work, determination, and dedication. Remember all things are possible for those who believe."

Gail Devers

Section 1

The Price of Greatness

Greatness is costly! It must cost you something precious and valuable. In economics, opportunity cost can be defined as not enjoying the benefit that would be had by taking the second best choice available. The New Oxford American Dictionary defines it as "the loss of potential gain from other alternatives when one alternative is chosen". On the Journey to greatness, there will be several opportunity costs, many sacrifices, loss of relationships and untold hardships. But to attain the prize, one must keep pressing on towards the goal. The journey to greatness requires heading towards the single vision set ahead. The vision must include a roadmap to where you are going and when you want to get there. One of the ways to do this is setting goals, identifying helpers, strategy and a consistent prayer life.

You cannot build great structures and affect people without an effective prayer life. We are not wrestling against flesh and blood, but against principalities and powers in high places. One of the reasons why we must pray as we plan, is because when there is no prayer, the people that are supposed to be impacted by your greatness become prey to the works of the evil or do not have access to your ministry. Prayer averts the plans of the devil; and it is a way of establishing ones dependence on Christ.

Greatness is intentional, and a price must be paid to attain it. This requires a plan, strategy and discipline.

Plan

- o Where are I am going?
- o When am I going to get there?

Strategy

- o Set goals

- o Become proficient in the pursuit of your goals
- o Strive to become great at what you do
- o Have a mentor
- o Invest time and resources in the pursuit of your goals.

Discipline

- o Time Management
- o Maintaining an enabling environment
- o Building right relationships
- o Live by design not be default
- o Times of mediations and reflections

Section 2

Wealth, Influence and Authority

Greatness brings a person into wealth, influence and authority even without seeking to be seen in that light. When a person knows the reasons for possessing wealth, influence and authority, they are effective tools in the hands of God to make other people's lives better and to serve their generation.

In Gen 1:28-29, God blessed man and said to them "Be fruitful and multiply, and fill the earth, and subdue it; and rule over the fish of the sea and over the birds of the sky and over every living thing that moves on the earth." Then God said, "Behold, I have given you every plant yielding seed that is on the surface of all the earth, and every tree which has fruit yielding seed; it shall be food for you."

When God created man, He blessed him as seen in Genesis 1:28, and gave him the mandate of fruitfulness, multiplying, having dominion and subduing the land. This shows that every person is blessed to live in abundance and live a wealthy lifestyle. However, as outlined in previous chapters, there is a land that is meant to be discovered to make fruitful, multiply, subdue and dominate. This can also be referred to as purpose.

There was a little city and few men within it, and there came a great king against it, and built great bulwarks against it: Now there was found in it a poor wise man and he by his wisdom delivered the city; yet no man remembered the poor man Then said I, Wisdom is better than strength; nevertheless the poor man's wisdom is despised, and his words are not heard.

Without wealth, wisdom is despised and it becomes difficult to create impact. The poor man had wisdom to deliver the city, but his words were not heard. The Bible says "Money answers all things" and I add this saying "Things answer to money." It is a lot easier to create impact with wealth. Some things, problems and situations, will only be resolved by wealth and riches.

Wealth is a reward of purpose and a characteristic of greatness. God spoke extensively about the four principles of wealth in several scriptures in the Bible.

1. The power to get wealth.
2. The principle of seed time and harvest time.
3. Diligence and faithfulness in work.
4. The wealth of nations.

Principle 1: The Power to Get Wealth

God is the owner and giver of wealth, "But remember the lord your God because he gives the power to get wealth, that He may confirm His covenant which He swore to His father's as it is today.

Physicists define power as the rate in which work is done or in which energy is transferred. This means that if power to get wealth is given, then the rate at which any work can be done is influenced by wealth. With money, a 10 story building can be erected in one year or less, while the reverse could take a decade. Hence, the speed of how much you achieve is influenced by God bestowing the power to get wealth for impact.

Some people believe that wealth is not for Christians. It is a misconception, a fallacy and a lie of the devil. Expect wealth, pray for it, envision and work towards it. It is your right as a child of God and it is needed for your destiny.

Principle 2: Sowing and reaping

Wealth is built on the principle of sowing and reaping. Seeds are lifeless objects that have the potential to produce great trees when placed in the soil. One of the principles of life states that what a man sows, that will he also reap. Seeds can come in different forms. It could be in money, acts of service, or kindness. When a seed is placed in the ground, it grows in the soil in which it was placed and will become a plant whose fruits will be harvested. We sow seeds daily through our actions, deeds and words; there is also a time to harvest the seeds that are sown in the ground.

Personally, whenever I find myself in a challenging situation, I sow a seed because I want to reap a harvest. There was a time in my life when I was struggling to get a job after completing my graduate schools secondary to several challenges beyond my control, I then emptied my bank account by faith paying tithe on the job I did not have. Within that month God responded by removing all the obstacles on my way and I was able to gain employment. God is the giver of a harvest, and through hard work, he crowns man with success and the ability to enjoy it. This is truly the gift of God.

"As for every man to whom God has given riches and wealth, and given him power to eat of it, to receive his heritage and rejoice in his labor--this is the gift of God." ECCLESIASTES 5:19

Principle 3: Diligence And Faithfulness

Diligence and faithfulness are attributes of God. These characteristics, in the life of a person, will always make the person attractive to others because of the dependability of the services rendered.

Diligence

Diligence can be characterized by showing great care and concern about the pursuit of something. A popular saying rightfully states that, "Many caves were only discovered after a diligent search". When we work diligently towards the pursuit of goals and purpose, we discover new things and ideas which will add value to the services we are rendering. Diligent people are sort after by the great men of the land because of the level in which they deliver services and the level of insight they possess. In the book Outliers by Malcom Gladwell, he talks about to become proficient at a skill, one must put in 10,000 hours to excel at a task, and how diligence in practice will yield greater results than natural talent. To attain a vision one must be diligent; this requires self-motivation because one might get to the end of the road without anyone else to believe in the attainment of that vision.

Faithfulness

Faithfulness is the ability to stay on task with an assignment, despite obstacles and challenges. As you proceed towards your goals, many things will come to test your commitment. Stay on task! That is the key to completing every goal.

As you proceed toward your goals, you might be working in a capacity to serve others. It is very important to work for them, like we would do for ourselves. Our God is faithful, and we appreciate the effect that his faithfulness has on us. We can rely upon him, so we ought to be reliable also.

God expects us to be faithful to Him, and He seeks men and women who will live so as to consistently carry out His will. Faithfulness to God with our wealth and resources shows our heart. Where your treasures lie, so will your heart also. "He that is faithful in that which is least is faithful also in much: and he that is unjust in the least is unjust also in much. If therefore, ye have not been faithful in the unrighteous mammon, who will commit to your trust the true riches? And if ye have not been faithful in that which is another man's, who shall give you that which is your own?"

Faithfulness is a virtue that transcends though different facets of our life, a person who is faithful in little things will be faithful in big things. A person who is unfaithful with keeping work time commitment will also be unfaithful in keeping other commitments in their lives. We become a product of our consistent actions!

A person who is unfaithful at his place of work and pockets little amounts of money will one day faithfully steal bigger amounts. The core of who we are is based on what we consistently do and refuse to do.

Principle 5: The wealth of nations

The wealth of the nations is laid up for the righteous. The riches of the world are the inheritance of the church. So why don't we have it? One of the reasons I have discovered is that we plan too small. Many of our business plans and ideas are limited to cities and countries. We ought to plan globally. Jesus said, "Go into the world and preach the gospel to every nation". I believe when we render services and ideas on a global level, we are preaching to the world about our God who has given us wisdom to acquire wealth.

Adam Smith, one of the greatest economist stated that the cause of increase in national wealth is labor, rather than the nation's quantity of gold or silver. The more spread out a company is in and its ability to utilize labor, the larger the lead to an increase in wealth. A good example of this is Wal-Mart. (See the greatness bites for more about the Wal-Mart Corporation

Section 4:
GREATNESS BITES

We save money so people can live better

Wal-Mart's mission

Sam Walton, is American businessman and founder of Wal-Mart, one of the largest global retail companies in the world, known for its low and affordable prices. The first Wal-Mart was opened in 1962 and has expanded internationally, growing into the world's largest company.

"If we work together, we'll lower the cost of living for everyone…we'll give the world an opportunity to see what it's like to save and have a better life."

He was also very involved in satisfying the workers, to provide them a better quality of life. He established an open door and a servant leadership policy to cater for the needs of his staff and customers and thus his corporation grew and continued to make great profit.

BITES FROM HIS LIFE

- He solved a problem for people by providing low prices.
- He expanded his business globally.
- He placed emphasis on satisfying his employees.
- He trained his leaders to serve.

- He placed great emphasis on customer service.

Section 5: Action Points

Write your story of the greatness, prophesy and write what you want to begin to see in your life now. Write about the great story that you want people to read about you, think about how God`s mighty hand will led you to positions that you never dreamt of, open up your imaginations and let the holy spirit connect you to the depth of God`s heart.

Tools to open up your spirit to the world of greatness

- Spending time reading the word of God and let the word become alive as you hear and speak them aloud.
- Listen to worship music, God is attracted to the fragrance of worship.
- Spend times in solitude intentionally and reflect on his works.
- Spend time with likeminded people.

- Find a mentor.
- Become a person of prayer.
- I will read about global trends in area of identified purpose.
- I will research several ways to serve my generation with my purpose.

Section I

Workbook

Section II Contents

If there is no passion in your life, then have you really lived? Find your passion, whatever it may be. Become it, and let it become you and you will find great things happen FOR you, TO you and BECAUSE of you.

T. ALAN ARMSTRONG

CHAPTER 1

ACTIVITY 1
THE JOURNEY: Reflections of the process

- What are my core values?
- List your ten core values in significant order?
- Do my closest friends have the same values?
- How can my environment enable my core values?
- When I die how do I want to be remembered?
- How am I working towards this vision of how I want to be remembered?
- How do I create time for this vision?
- What are the limiting factors that prevent me?
- Am I comfortable with making the necessary adjustments?

Activity 3: Personal Inventory Checklist

You have been wired for an assignment. Let`s take inventory of your gifts, interests, talents and aspirations.

Interests	Habits	Talents	Skills	Aspirations

Activity 4: Frame of Reference

G.R.E.A.T	**AREA OF FOCUS**	**PLAN**	**GOAL**
GROWTH *What will you do to improve?*			
REASONS *Why am I doing this?*			
ENERGY *How will I stay energized with the source of my strength?*			
ACQUIRE *What do I need?*			
TREASURE *What do I have and what do I need to achieve my vision?*			

Activity 4: SWOT Analysis

S.W.O.T This instrument can be used as a tool to analyze personal growth in an area or components of a goal	
STRENGTHS	
WEAKNESSES	
OPPORTUNITIES	
THREATS	

Activity 5
MAPPING OUT YOUR GREATNESS

Write the vision, make it plain that he that reads it will run with it".

What have I done with my life thus far?

____

____

____

____

____

One Year Plan:

____

____

____

____

____

Five-Year Plan:

____

____

____

Ten-Year Plan:

Twenty-Year Plan:

Fifty Year Plan:

What Work Will Continue After I Die?

Activity 6

Compassion Trails
Passions
What arouses you? What triggers emotions in you?
Affection
What are the things you don't need motivation to do?
Burdens
What problems do you want to solve?
Revelation
What pictures, instructions or words has God shown you?
Potentials
What are your gifts and talents?
Wisdom
What areas do you possess deep insight?
Family Identity
What trends do you see success in your family background?
Experience
What positive or negative events shape your life?

Activity 7: Greatness: Purpose, Passion & Power

Purpose: Gives meaning to life.

Passion: Gives joy and fulfillment

Power : Ability to do work

Action points

1. Name three activities that you currently do or want to start that engage all three of those components.

2. Start finding people with similar interests.

Activity 8: Definitive life Assignment

A person might have several assignments and purpose for every stage of life but there is one life assignment that gives birth to the other ones.

For example, Oprah is a TV talk show host and channel owner which has enabled her to become a Philanthropist.

In the previous activity 7, we named three things that we believe engage our purpose, passion and power.

Now think of which of those things can fund or can serve as the umbrella to the other assignments. That is the definitive life assignment.

Spend time using the G.R.E.A.T frame of reference to understand it.

Activity 9: Personality Tests

This activity will help one identify strengths and weaknesses of one's personality as well as identify possible niches.

Type	Characteristics	Niches
Sensing (S) + Judging (J) SJ - The "Protector	Protectors (SJs) are dependable, altruistic and honest. They are driven by a strict work ethic and place a high premium on helping others and serving the community. Protectors are gifted leaders because of their natural ability to organize, plan and strategize. They thrive in situations where they know what is expected of them.	Typical Career Matches: Police, Military, Accountant, Administrator, Judge Famous SJ People: George Washington, Queen Elizabeth II, Warren Buffet, Sam Walton, Harry Truman SJ Personality Types: ESTJ Overseer, ESFJ Supporter, ISTJ Examiner, ISFJ Defender
Sensing (S) + Perceiving (P) SP - The	Creators (SPs) are naturally artistic, brave and adaptable. They appreciate the beauty in nature, fashion and	Typical Career Matches: Musician, Pilot, Photographer, Detective, Paramedic, Athlete Famous SP People:

"Creator"	decoration. Their adventurous nature makes them excitable, energetic and spontaneous. Driven by their curiosity and playfulness, Creators are willing to try almost anything. They are likable and popular as they love to tell a good story or joke.	Barbara Streisand, Bill Clinton, Mozart, Michael Jordan, Jacqueline Kennedy SP Personality Types: ESTP Persuader, ESFP Entertainer, ISTP Craftsman, ISFP Artist
Intuitive (N) + Thinking (T) NT – The Intellectual	Intellectuals (NTs) are intelligent, independent and determined. They are high-achievers, driven not only to acquire but also to master large amounts of information. They are self-sufficient, logical and value reasoning. While Intellectuals have a desire to know everything, they also	Typical Career Matches: Engineer, Scientist, Psychologist, Lawyer, Inventor Famous NT People: Albert Einstein, Bill Gates, Margaret Thatcher, Socrates Fictional NT Characters: Kramer (Seinfeld), Data (Star Trek), Gandalf (Lord of the Rings) NT Personality Types: ENTJ Chief, ENTP Originator, INTJ

	tend to question anything. Their keen interest in investigation and questioning make them great researchers and inventors.	Strategist, INTP Engineer
Intuitive (N) + Feeling (F)	Visionaries (NFs) are empathetic, generous and original. They are caring individuals who are not only sensitive to the feelings of others but also very adept at identifying them. They are idealistic and are driven by values they deeply believe in and defend. Visionaries desire to understand themselves and to be understood for who they really are.	Typical Career Matches: Therapist, Social Worker, Teacher, Writer, Activist Famous NF People: Albert Schweitzer, Princess Diana, Dr. Seuss, Martin Luther King Jr., Charles Dickens NF Personality Types: ENFJ Mentor, ENFP Advocate, INFJ Confidant, INFP Dreamer

Culled from paramount assessments

Temperament and Personality Assessment.

Sanguine	***Choleric***	**Melancholy**	***Phlegmatic***
Joyful/Cheerful Optimistic Passionate Outgoing/Attention-seeking Responsive to emotions Charismatic Compassionate Impractical/Dreamer Storyteller Childlike Memory for smells & colors Makes friends easily Doesn't hold grudges Loves people Inattention Lack of concentration Disorganization	Self-sufficient Born leader Dynamic Practical Compulsive need for change Must correct wrongs Unemotional Strong-willed Independent Optimistic Not discouraged easily Confident Goal-oriented Knows the right answers Can see the whole picture Quickly moves to action Thrives on opposition Little need for friends Leads and organizes Excels in emergencies	Sensitive to anguish of others Analytical Deep thinker Self-introspective Artistic or musical Self-sacrificing Poetic and philosophical Appreciates beauty Perfectionist with high standards Detail conscious Neat and tidy Organized Sees the problem Seeks creative solutions Must finish what is started Content to stay behind the scenes Likes charts, numbers, and lists Cautious to make friends Problem solver for others	Calm and collected Quiet Witty Sympathetic Kind Inoffensive Hides emotions Reconciled to life Not in a hurry Takes the good with the bad Practical Dry sense of humor Mediator Avoids confrontation and conflict Cool under pressure Takes the easiest way Good listener Likes to watch

Easily distracted Forgetful Impulsive Restless Very talkative Interrupts (Egotistical) Weak-willed Emotionally unstable Unpredictable Circumstantial	Delegates work Motivator Long-term thinker Hot-tempered Cruel Impetuous Impatient	Moved to tears with compassion Tries not to raise attention Serious Conscientious Studious Reflective Not practical-- Dreamer Self-centered Pessimistic Moody Revengeful Skeptical	people Compassionate and concerned Pleasant Good administrative ability Intuitive Dependable Efficient Slow and Lazy Teaser/Sarcastic Selfish Stubborn Indecisive Detached observer

Culled from Spirit filled temperaments

Activity 10: Covenant of Greatness

COVENANT OF GREATNESS
I, ____________________ am enlisting in God's army to bring life to the nations through my purpose. I am committed to discovering God's purpose for my life; my greatness is inevitable as I strategically map out steps and plans to carry out God's plan as a covenant to establish the earth. The grace of God is empowering me today to do what eyes have not seen, ears have heard and man has not conceived. I sign this contract today as a generational covenant that I will teach my children and everyone around I can mentor to work in this wisdom. I am now a person of value so I walk in holiness as I attract the power of God to do great works through me. As for my household and me we are partnering with Jehovah to live out God's purpose on this earth as the only map to greatness as we become committed to hearing and obeying the voice of God. As I do this, God will make me great with wealth, wisdom and influence to make a difference in my world.
Date:
Spouse/Accountability Partner (signature):

AUTHOR'S REFLECTION

In 2006, God redirected my journey at Urbana, a Christian student conference organized by the Intervarsity Christian fellowship. Prior to that conference I was a social Christian whose limited understanding about God was an image of a Santa Claus who gave me gifts. However, the theme of the conference was "I Have a Calling, There is a Purpose for My Life" and for those four days I could not stop crying because for the first time ever, I understood that God had a plan for me and it involved me having a relationship with him.

This was so strategic because I had just completed my Bachelors degree that month, and was starting to apply to graduate school. This shaped my decision to pursue a Masters Degree in Occupational Therapy, which has empowered me for my purpose.

Seven years later and many mountains climbed, the plan still unfolds and it is very certain that God is not Santa Claus, but a Father who freely gives us all of Himself, which includes assignments and responsibilities.

Just like fathers on earth have great expectations and reward their children based on their achievement, God does more than that, He rewards, bestows and even has mercy! He wants to bring us to our expected end, which is greatness. However, there is a role that the will of a man will play in his destiny.

Every man must be willing to drown out the voice of the public or popular opinions to follow God's agenda. The journey might not be a smooth sail. There will be waves and turbulence along the way, but we must prevail and push through with hard work and prayer just like the people in the days of Nehemiah who held the sword in one hand and the trowel in the other as they rebuilt the wall.

We are co-creators of our destiny. Generations are awaiting your greatness!

References

REFERENCES

Doll, Joy. Program Development and Grant Writing in Occupational therapy. MA: Jones and Bartlett , 2010.
Attwood J. D & Attwood C.A. The effortless path to discovering your life purpose. MA: Penguin, 2008.
Frost, Bob. *John D. Rockefeller: Infinitely Ruthless, Profoundly Charitable. 2000.* Retrieved 5.12.2013 from http://historyaccess.com/johnd.rockefella.html.

The origin of the redeemed chrisitian church 2007. Retrieved 4.21.2013 from http://rccgvh.org/origin.html
Perry, Tyler biography, retrieved 3.11.2013 from http://www.biography.com/people/tylerperry-361274

The Religion of Scientists
Part 2: Great Scientists Who Believe. Retrieved

5.12.2013 from
http://www.english.sdaglobal.org/research/sctst bel.htm

The Religious Affiliation of Rocket Engineer and Inventor Wernher von Braun retrieved on 5.19.2013 from
http://www.adherents.com/people/pv/Wernher_von_Braun.html

Faraday, Michael profile retrieved 6.14.2013 from http://www.nndb.com/people/571/000024499/

Compass. Retrieved 3.11.13 from

http://en.wikipedia.org/wiki/Compass

http://www.kingjamesbibleonline.org

Farfan, Barbara. Wal-Mart`s stores mission. Retrieved 9.2.2014 from
http://retailindustry.about.com/od/retailbestpractices/ig/Company-Mission-Statements/WalMart-Mission-Statement.htm

www.ingramcontent.com/pod-product-compliance
Lightning Source LLC
Chambersburg PA
CBHW072007040426
42447CB00009B/1520
* 9 7 8 0 6 1 5 8 8 5 8 7 2 *